DISCIPLE
notebook

Also by Fr. Mark Goring, CC

- In His Zone
  7 Principles for Thriving in Solitude

- St. Joseph the Protector
  A Nine-day Preparation for Entrustment to St. Joseph

DISCIPLE
notebook

Foundations
Living in the Spirit
Evangelization

Fr. Mark Goring, CC
2019

 COMPANIONS OF THE CROSS

199 Bayswater Avenue
Ottawa, ON K1Y 2G5
Canada

http://www.companionscross.org

1949 Cullen Blvd
Houston TX 77023
USA

DISCIPLE *notebook*

By Fr. Mark Goring, CC

© 2017, 2018, 2019. Companions of the Cross.

All right reserved.

Paintings, cover design, layout: Sr. Penelope Nguyen, SC

    "The Gardener" on the front cover

    "Proverbs 6:6" on the back cover

ISBN 978-1539980773

To
Fr. Francis Frankovich, CC

CONTENTS

- Fr Tito
- Fr Murray

- Fr Joe keefe

Welcome

Thank you for responding to the Lord's call to be His disciple!

The Discipleship series is meant to be taken in the context of dedicating a year to growing closer to the Lord. At the beginning of His ministry, the Lord declared "**the acceptable year of the Lord**" (Luke 4:19 RSV).

The most important commitment for the year is daily personal prayer. We call this THE ONE THING. Jesus told Martha: "**There is need of only one thing. Mary has chosen the better part and it will not be taken from her**" (Luke 10:42 NAB). Mary was sitting at the feet of Jesus, listening to His Words and giving Him her undivided attention.

Another essential component of the year is daily Scripture reading. Jesus said: "**If you remain in my word, you will truly be my disciples...**" (John 8:31 NAB).

May you truly be His disciples this year and forever!

Fr. Mark Goring, CC
Catholic Charismatic Center, Director

Cell Group

An important component of the Discipleship Year is being part of a small group or "**Cell Group.**"

Healthy organisms grow because they are made up of small cells that multiply. This is how the church is meant to grow. We call this "spiritual multiplication."

2 Timothy 2:2 *And what you heard from me through many witnesses entrust to faithful people who will have the ability to teach others as well.*

And here are some suggestions for Cell Groups (CG):

1. There is no strict rule for the number of people in a CG. One recommendation is 3-6 people.

2. Towards the beginning of every discipleship class, CG's should have a "check-in."

3. "Check-in" is a time for each member of the CG to share how one's week has been going especially regarding the disciplines of: prayer, Scripture reading, gratitude and growing in virtue.

4. After the teaching, CG members share their thoughts and reflections regarding the teaching.

5. CG members can pray together or over each other before the class ends.

6. It is important that no one dominates the CG by doing all or most of the talking. Everyone should be given the opportunity to speak.

7. CG members should keep one another in prayer throughout the week.

FOUNDATIONS

*A parish which invested in training
just five authentic lay apostles
would be assured of at least thirty or
forty years of loyal service,
right up to death.
How much potential we leave unseen
and untapped in the kingdom of God.*

– Cardinal Francis Xavier Nguyen Van Thuan

Prayer

"Prayer is the best weapon we have;
it is the key to God's heart."

— St. Pio of Pietrelcina

Scriptures

Psalms 1:3 He is like a tree planted near streams of water, that yields its fruit in season; Its leaves never wither; whatever he does prospers.

Revelation 22:2 On either side of the river grew the tree of life that produces fruit twelve times a year, once each month; the leaves of the trees serve as medicine for the nations.

John 4:10, 13-14 Jesus answered and said to her, "If you knew the gift of God and who is saying to you, 'Give me a drink,' you would have asked him and he would have given you living water...." Jesus answered and said to her, "Everyone who drinks this water will be thirsty again; but whoever drinks the water I shall give will never thirst; the water I shall give will become in him a spring of water welling up to eternal life."

Exodus 16:19-21 Moses said to them, "Let no one leave any of it over until morning." But they did not listen to Moses, and some kept a part of it over until morning, and it became wormy and stank. Therefore, Moses was angry with them. Morning after morning they gathered it, as much as each needed to eat; but when the sun grew hot, it melted away.

Wisdom 16:20, 27-28 Instead of this, you nourished your people with food of angels and furnished them bread from heaven, ready to hand, untoiled for, endowed with all delights and conforming to every taste. For what was not destroyed by fire, melted when merely warmed by a momentary sunbeam; To make known that one must give you thanks before sunrise, and turn to you at daybreak.

Mark 1:35 Rising very early before dawn, he left and went off to a deserted place, where he prayed.

Psalms 23:2 In green pastures he makes me lie down; to still waters he leads me.

Key Points

1. We are not just followers of Jesus; we are His disciples.

2. Disciple implies disciplines and habits, a way of life.

3. Establishing a discipline of prayer is like planting a tree.

4. Jesus wants to give us Living Water; a tree needs water.

5. When we pray, we are gathering our daily manna.

6. A shepherd needs to find clean water for his sheep. The morning dew is the best water.

7. Our daily prayer time should be in the same place, at the same time, and have a consistent structure.

Practical Application

1. Some of the most successful Catholics with great responsibilities pray an hour a day, usually early in the morning.

2. Fruits of prayer include: serenity, peace, joy, clarity, wisdom, sober intoxication and salvation.

3. "Those who pray are certainly saved."
   - St. Liguori, CCC 2744

Discussion Questions

1. Do you have a daily time of personal prayer?

2. What are some of your prayer disciplines?

3. How do you try to keep your communion with the Lord throughout the day?

Homework

o If you do not have a prayer journal, purchase a notebook to be used as a prayer journal.

o Establish a place, time & structure for daily prayer in your life. Begin with 20 minutes.

Scripture

*"The Church has always venerated
the divine Scriptures as she venerates
the Body of the Lord"*

— *(Dei Verbum 21, quoted in CCC #141)*

Scriptures

Hebrews 4:12 Indeed, the word of God is living and effective, sharper than any two-edged sword, penetrating even between soul and spirit, joints and marrow, and able to discern reflections and thoughts of the heart.

Isaiah 55:10-11 Yet just as from the heavens the rain and snow come down and do not return there, till they have watered the earth, making it fertile and fruitful, giving seed to the one who sows and bread to the one who eats, so shall my word be that goes forth from my mouth; It shall not return to me empty, but shall do what pleases me, achieving the end for which I send it.

John 6:63 It is the spirit that gives life, while the flesh is of no avail. The words I have spoken to you are spirit and life.

Mark 4:3, 14 A sower went out to sow… The sower sows the word.

Jeremiah 15:16 When I found your words, I devoured them; your words were my joy, the happiness of my heart.

Matthew 4:4 He said in reply, "It is written: 'One does not live by bread alone, but by every word that come forth from the mouth of God.'"

Psalms 119:105 Your word is a lamp for my feet, a light for my path.

Luke 10:42 There is need of only one thing. Mary has chosen the better part and it will not be taken from her.

Key Points

1. Jesus is present in His Word.

2. God's Word is more than just inspiring; it has power!

3. Our living and our thinking should line up with God's Word.

4. God's Word should become part of our interior life. Our mind, heart and soul should be filled with God's Word.

5. When we teach, preach and evangelize, we should make God's Word the foundation of our message.

6. We should spend our whole life studying God's Word.

7. We don't memorize God's Word; we learn it by heart.

Practical Application

1. St. Therese of Lisieux, St. Francis always tried to confirm insights with passages from the Bible.

2. Most ancient way of prayer: Read and listen.

Discussion Questions

1. Have you fallen in love with God's Word?

2. Have you ever experienced the extraordinary power of God's Word? Share your experience.

3. How are you inspired after listening to this talk? Would you adjust your daily prayer to include a period of praying with God's Word?

Homework

o   Ask the Lord for the grace of loving His Word.

o   Every day, spend a few minutes reading and praying with the Scriptures during your prayer time.

o   Learn by heart one Scripture passage this week.

Journaling

*"A spiritual journal is related to
my time of personal prayer,
my daily quiet time with the Lord."*

— *Fr. Bob Bedard, CC*

Scriptures

Habakkuk 2:2 Then the LORD answered me and said: "Write down the vision; Make it plain upon tablets, so that the one who reads it may run."

Psalms 36:10 For with you is the fountain of life, and in your light we see light.

John 10:27 My sheep hear my voice; I know them, and they follow me.

Key Points

1. Good students take notes.

28

2. How to Journal:

    a. Record the date in your journal. If you travel a lot, you may also want to record your location.

    b. Have a typical entry that you make each day. For example, you may want to write three things for which you are grateful.

    c. Use your journal to record any important info such as: Scriptures, insights, questions, prayers, resolutions, drawings, etc.

    d. Occasionally review what you have written in you journal.

Seven images

1. Adventure journal: life is journey –record milestones – gratitude.

2. Student's notebooks: most important lessons.

3. Lab journal: record data as we experiment.

4. Legal document: paper trail proving we asked for God's wisdom and help.

5. Sign in book: accountability.

6. Diary: process feelings.

7. Symbol: Faith that God speaks.

Discussion Questions

1. Have you ever kept a prayer journal?

2. Do you find it helpful to write things down?

3. Which journal image do you like the most?

Homework

o   If you have not done so already, purchase a notebook to be used as a prayer journal.

o   Begin making journaling a part of your daily prayer time.

o   Decide what your entry will be.

Gratitude

*"No duty is more urgent than that
of returning thanks."*
— St. Ambrose

Scriptures

Nehemiah 8:10 Today is holy to our Lord. Do not be
saddened this day, for rejoicing in the Lord is your
strength!

1 Thessalonians 5:16-18 Rejoice always. Pray without
ceasing. In all circumstances give thanks.

Psalms 100:4 Enter his gates with thanksgiving, his
courts with praise.

Philippians 4:8 Finally, brothers, whatever is true,
whatever is pure, whatever is lovely, whatever is
gracious, if there is any excellence and if there is
anything worthy of praise, think about these things.

Exodus 16:2-3 Here in the wilderness the whole Israelite
community grumbled against Moses and Aaron. The
Israelites said to them, "If only we had died at the Lord's
hand in the land of Egypt, as we sat by our kettles of meat

and ate our fill of bread! But you have led us into this wilderness to make this whole assembly die of famine!"

James 1:17 ...every perfect gift is from above, coming down from the Father of lights...

Matthew 5:8 Blessed are the pure of heart, for they will see God.

Romans 8:28 (RSV) We know that in everything God works for good with those who love Him...

Proverbs 18:21 Death and life are in the power of the tongue.

Key Points

1. We need to adopt an 'attitude of gratitude.' Gratitude should be a way of life.

2. The devil is negative; God is positive.

3. Our God is a God who gives. He is constantly pouring out blessings in our lives.

4. Gratitude is one of the best ways to live in the presence of God and to exercise faith.

5. Grumbling is a serious sin against faith.

6. Being positive and having an attitude of gratitude is a decision, a discipline, and should become a habit. Being positive rewires our brain in a positive way.

7. Our speech is extremely important and has a huge impact on ourselves and on others. We are made in the image of God and what we speak, in some way, comes to be.

8. No one likes to be around a negative person. It is often better to remain silent than to say something negative.

9. Sometimes we do need to speak the truth, even if it might sound like we are being negative. We need to adopt a 'positive realism.'

Practical Application

1. Develop the habit of giving thanks to the Lord at certain time in your day. For example: when waking up, when driving your car, when dining with family…

2. Find playful, joyful and positive phrases to speak into your life:

    − God is good!
    − I'm so blessed it's embarrassing!
    − I'm having too much fun!

Discussion Questions

1. Share your own experience of being grateful.

2. Have you had special seasons of gratitude in your life?

3. Have you had times when thinking positive has saved you from falling into despair and hopelessness?

Homework

- o Every day in your journal write three things for which you are grateful.

- o Review today's teaching during one of your prayer times.

- o Try to observe yourself this week and see if you are sometimes negative.

Virtue

*"To defend his purity, Saint Francis of Assisi
rolled in the snow, Saint Benedict threw himself
into a thorn bush, and Saint Bernard plunged
into an icy pond... You – what have you done?"*
— *St. Josemaria Escriva*

Scriptures

1 Peter 1:16 for it is written, "Be holy because I am
holy."

Matthew 23:26 Blind Pharisee, cleanse first the inside
of the cup, so that the outside also may be clean.

Matthew 7:21 Not everyone who says to me, "Lord,
Lord," will enter the kingdom of heaven, but only the one
who does the will of my Father in heaven.

Romans 8:13 For if you live according to the flesh, you
will die, but if by the spirit you put to death the deeds of
the body, you will live.

Wisdom 12:2, 10 Therefore, you rebuke offenders little by little… But condemning them by degrees, you gave them space for repentance.

Mark 4:26-27 …the kingdom of God; it is as if a man were to scatter seed on the land and would sleep and rise night and day and the seed would sprout and grow, he knows not how.

John 15:1-2 I am the true vine, and my Father is the vine grower. He takes away every branch in me that does not bear fruit, and everyone that does he prunes so that it bears more fruit.

Key Points

1. If you want to change your life, change your habits.

2. One small change can have a huge positive ripple effect in our life.

3. The Holy Spirit loves to show us what we need to change in our life.

4. If God asks us to change something, He will give us the grace and power to make that change.

5. We need to be patient and persevere. Most things grow slowly.

6. Virtue always brings true happiness; what is called "beatitude."

7. Making lasting changes in our life gives us hope.

8. Making small lasting changes in our life is a painfully slow process but it works. This is the classic way of growing in virtue.

Monthly Change

1. Experts say it takes between 21-40 days to either break the power of a bad habit or establish a good habit. The easiest approach is to simply **work on one small change in our life each month.**

2. At the beginning of each month, ask the Holy Spirit to show you what change He is asking you to make by praying *the "Small Change Prayer"* below.

3. We need God's strength and power if we wish to grow in virtue. We should always rely on the power of the Holy Spirit. We might want to pray the *"Freedom Prayer"* each day to receive God's grace.

Small Change Prayer

Holy Spirit, what is the one small change
You are giving me the grace to make
this month, that will have the biggest positive
effect in my life?

(Note: Pray this prayer during your time of journaling
and write down the change you feel the Lord
is calling you to make.)

Freedom Prayer

Lord Jesus Christ, Son of God, have mercy on me a
sinner. You promised Lord that You would set the
captives free. I confess Jesus that I am a slave and only
You can break that chains that bind me. I repent of
relying on my own strength. Without You Jesus I can
do nothing. I ask You Lord Jesus to set me free from
(name area in your life where you need freedom).
Come Holy Spirit and clothe me with power
from on high (take a moment and allow the Holy Spirit
to empower you). Give me the grace Lord Jesus to walk
in faith today, confident in Your love and mercy. Amen.

Discussion Questions

1. Do you sometimes feel that you are stuck in the spiritual life?

2. What is a weakness with which you struggle?

3. Has there been a weakness that you've overcome in your life? How were you set free?

Homework

○ In your journal, write a list of changes you could make in your life.

○ Ask the Holy Spirit to show you what one small change He is asking you to make right now.

LIVING
IN THE SPIRIT

Be filled with the knowledge of his will through all spiritual wisdom and understanding to live in a manner worthy of the Lord, so as to be fully pleasing, in every good work bearing fruit and growing in the knowledge of God, strengthened with every power, in accord with his glorious might, for all endurance and patience, with joy giving thanks to the Father, who has made you fit to share in the inheritance of the holy ones in light. He delivered us from the power of darkness and transferred us to the kingdom of his beloved Son, in whom we have redemption, the forgiveness of sins.

– Colossians 1:9-14

Praise

Oh hear the angel voices!
— "Oh, Holy Night" Christmas hymn

Scriptures

Psalms 34:2 I will bless the Lord at all times; his praise shall be always in my mouth.

Psalms 100:1-2, 4 Shout joyfully to the Lord, all you lands; serve the Lord with gladness; come before him with joyful song… Enter his gates with thanksgiving, his courts with praise.

Psalms 103:1 Bless the Lord, my soul; all my being, bless his holy name!

Psalms 113:3 From the rising of the sun to its setting, let the name of the Lord be praised.

Psalms 150:6 Let everything that has breath give praise to the Lord! Hallelujah!

Revelation 4:1, 8 I had a vision of an open door to heaven… Day and night they do not stop exclaiming:

"Holy, holy, holy is the Lord God almighty, who was, and who is, and who is to come."

Key Points

1. It's good to affirm people.

2. The truth will set you free.

3. We were made to praise God for all eternity.

4. If you love to praise God in this life, it's a sign of where you will spend eternity.

5. Praise leads to worship. Worship leads to adoration. Adoration leads to contemplation.

6. Praise is not a feeling; it's a decision but also a gift.

Points to Ponder

1. We offer to God a sacrifice of praise. This is the work of God's people. This is a way of life for religious communities.

2. Music is spiritual and powerful and is meant to give glory to God.

3. All of creation praises the Lord. We are called to enter into creation's rhythm of worship.

Discussion Questions

1. Do you like to praise the Lord?

2. Have you experienced an event where the worship was moving and powerful?

3. What do you find difficult about praising the Lord?

Homework

○ Use <u>Vocabulary of Praise</u> in this book starting on page 120 during your prayer time.

○ Praise the Lord throughout the day even when you don't feel like it.

○ Learn by heart one praise Scripture.

Listening Prayer

"The Lord wants us to tell him we will do whatever he wants no matter what it is. Abandonment to the will of God is the key."
— *Fr. Bob Bedard, CC*

Scriptures

John 10:27 My sheep hear my voice; I know them, and they follow me.

1 Samuel 3:10 Speak, for your servant is listening.

1 Corinthians 14:5 Now I should like all of you to speak in tongues, but even more to prophesy.

1 Samuel 23:4 Again David consulted the Lord, who answered: Go down to Keilah, for I will deliver the Philistines into your power.

John 14:26 The Advocate, the Holy Spirit that the Father will send in my name – he will teach you everything and remind you of all that I told you.

Hebrews 3:15 "Oh, that today you would hear His voice: 'Harden not your hearts as at the rebellion.'"

Key Points

1. David was very successful as a military leader. He repeatedly consulted the Lord for His "rhema" word – the "now" word.

2. God is real and personal and wants to communicate with us.

3. Like radio waves, we need to tune in to God's voice.

4. Like a sailor who can sense the changes in the wind.

5. Sometimes we get it wrong. We shouldn't be too quick to say: "God told me!" It's often better to say: "I sense the Lord might be saying…"

6. It's good to consult others when we feel we've heard from the Lord. God also speaks through the body and legitimate authority.

7. Get in touch with your feelings. God often uses our feelings as starting point when He wants to speak to us.

8. Peace is the litmus test.

Practical Application

1. Every day, during your prayer time, take a few moments to be still and listen to the Lord's still small voice in your heart. Write it down.

2. In your prayer journal, write questions to the Lord. Listen and write down possible answers that come to mind.

Discussion Questions

1. Find someone you don't know and ask the Lord for a word for that person. (Activity in pairs – each person takes 2 minutes asking God to give a word for the person, while other person intercedes for the person who is seeking the word.)

2. Can you share an example in your life where you felt the Lord spoke clearly and directly to you?

Homework

o   After praising the Lord during your prayer time,
     say to Him: "Speak Lord, your servant is
     listening." Then, be still and write down what
     you sense the Lord might be telling you.

Charisms

*"Be who God meant you to be
and you will set the world on fire!"*
— *St. Catherine of Siena*

Scriptures

1 Corinthians 12:7 (RSV) To each is given the manifestation of the Spirit for the common good.

1 Corinthians 12:4-5 There are different kinds of spiritual gifts but the same Spirit; there are different forms of service but the same Lord.

1 Corinthians 14:1 Strive eagerly for the spiritual gifts.

Matthew 25:25 …so out of fear I went off and buried your talent in the ground. Here it is back.

Luke 12:48 Much will be required of the person entrusted with much, and still more will be demanded of the person entrusted with more.

Psalms 20:5 May he grant what is in your heart, fulfill your every plan.

Matthew 2:9 And behold, the star that they had seen at its rising preceded them, until it came and stopped over the place where the child was.

1 Corinthians 12:14-15 Now the body is not a single part, but many. If a foot should say, "Because I am not a hand I do not belong to the body," it does not for this reason belong any less to the body.

Key Points

1. A charism is a Holy Spirit empowered ability.

2. Charisms (or spiritual gifts) are given to those who have personal relationship with the Lord.

3. Charisms are not for one's personal sanctification but for others. Charisms are gifts given to us to be used to build up the Church.

4. Those who minister in their charisms experience
    fruitfulness, joy and a sense of fulfillment. Those
    who try to minister outside their charism
    experience frustration.

5. If something grieves you (i.e. No one seems to be
    reaching out to the disabled in your church) it is
    often an indication of that to which the Lord is
    calling you.

6. It is possible to have a natural gift but lack a charism in that area. For example, music and teaching.

7. When we are operating in our charisms, people experience God.

8. In a church or community where all the charisms are in operation, Jesus is most fully manifested.

9. The Church and the world desperately need your particular manifestation of the Spirit.

Practical Application

1. List of 25 common charisms: administration, celibacy, craftsmanship, discernment of spirits, encouragement, evangelism, faith, giving, healing, helps, hospitality, intercessory prayer, knowledge, leadership, mercy, missionary, music, pastoring, prophecy, tongues, service, teaching, voluntary poverty, wisdom, and writing.

2. People often discover their charisms through trial and error. You can only steer a ship that is in motion.

Discussion Questions

1. What do you think might be one of your charisms?

2. What charism would you like?

3. What are some charisms that might not be as appreciated yet vitally important?

Homework

- o Read through the charisms list and prayerfully consider which three might be your top gifts.

- o In your journal, make a dream list of at least 10 things you would love to do for the Lord and His Kingdom.

Inner Healing

*"If a man finds it very hard to forgive injuries,
let him look at a Crucifix, and think that Christ
shed all His Blood for him, and not only forgave
His enemies, but even prayed for His Heavenly
Father to forgive them also.*

— *Saint Philip Neri*

Scriptures

Ezekiel 36:26 I will give you a new heart, and a new
spirit I will put within you. I will remove the heart of
stone from your flesh and give you a heart of flesh. I will
put my Spirit within you so that you walk in my
statutes...

Luke 23:34a Then Jesus said, "Father, forgive them,
they know not what they do."

Matthew 6:14ff If you forgive others their
transgressions, your heavenly Father will forgive you.

Romans 8:28 We know that all things work for good for those who love God.

Revelation 21:5 Behold, I make all things new.

Psalms 36:10 In your light, we see light.

Psalms 34:19 The Lord is close to the brokenhearted.

Key Points

1. Inner healing is a very broad topic.

2. Being hurt and needing to forgive and be healed is a universal experience.

3. Hurt people hurt people. Healed people heal people.

4. When a bad fruit appears, we need to ask ourselves: what is the root?

5. God wants to heal our wounded hearts.

6. We need to be reconciled with our past.

7. Inner healing, forgiveness and deliverance should be a way of life.

8. God wants to turn our test into a testimony. He wants to turn our mess into a message. He wants to turn our trial into a triumph.

9. People who have been healed by God have authority.

10. When we open our hearts to Jesus, He immediately begins to heal us.

Practical Application

These are the steps we need to take:

1. Enter into God's presence. Remain in God's presence.

2. Exercise faith and thank the Lord.

3. Repent and ask God to forgive you any wrongs you've committed.

4. Cover the hurtful experience from the past in prayer. You can imagine the Lord with you as you were being hurt. What was He feeling, thinking and doing?

5. Forgive the people who have hurt you. Ask the Lord to bless them. **FORGIVENESS IS THE KEY.**

6. Renounce any evil you may have allowed into your heart. And command the powers of darkness to be gone in the Name of Jesus.

7. Bring closure and get on with your life.

8. Proclaim your new story.

Discussion Questions

1. Are you familiar with the process of inner healing?

2. Do you have a story of forgiveness that you are comfortable to share?

3. Do you feel that the Lord is healing you and giving you a new heart?

Homework

- o During a prayer time, ask the Lord to show you anyone you need to forgive, especially the one person who is most hard to forgive.

- o During a prayer time, ask the Lord to show you any bad fruits that might be manifesting in your life.

Community

"Community is a sign that love is possible in a materialistic world where people so often either ignore or fight each other. It is a sign that we don't need a lot of money to be happy – in fact, the opposite."
— *Jean Vanier, Community and Growth*

Scriptures

Genesis 11:1, 9 The whole world had the same language and the same words... That is why it was called Babel, because there the Lord confused the speech of all the world. From there the Lord scattered them over all the earth.

Acts 2:5, 11 Now there were Jews from every nation under heaven staying in Jerusalem... we hear them speaking in our own tongues of the mighty acts of God.

Acts 2:42, 44 They devoted themselves to the teaching of the apostles and to the communal life, to the breaking of the bread and to the prayers… All who believed were together and had all things in common.

John 13:35 This is how all will know that you are my disciples, if you have love for one another.

Luke 8:1-3 He journeyed from one town and village to another, preaching and proclaiming the good news of the kingdom of God. Accompanying him were the Twelve and some women… and many others who provided for them out of their resources.

Matthew 18:20 For where two or three are gathered together in my name, there am I in the midst of them.

Hebrews 10:25 We should not stay away from our assembly.

Luke 14:13-14 Rather, when you hold a banquet, invite the poor, the crippled, the lame, the blind; blessed indeed will you be…

Key Points

1. God, the Holy Trinity, is a communion of love.

2. One of the fruits of any renewal in the Church is a desire among the faithful for community. Community is a work of the Spirit.

3. Community is an essential part of the Gospel. We are one body.

4. Authentic Christian community is a witness. It converts hearts.

5. We need to reach a degree of independence before we can truly become interdependent. Otherwise we become co-dependent.

6. Small Christian communities include prayer groups, Bible studies, lay associations, third order communities, study groups, Christian reading groups, men's groups, women's groups, share groups, and Bible lunch groups.

7. Some ministries are also a form of community. Authentic community requires some form of prayer and depth of sharing.

8. Christian community should be inclusive and members should be selfless.

9. We cannot do it on our own.

Practical Application

1. We should make an effort to be part of a small Christian community.

2. The purpose of community is to receive but also to give. Members should be committed.

3. Small Christian communities can range in size.

4. Members can meet weekly, twice a month or once a month.

5. Gathering time should include: Praise, Scripture, sharing and prayer.

Discussion Questions

1. Are you part of a small Christian community?

2. What kind of small Christian community appeals to you?

3. What do you think is the most important things that members of a small Christian community should do together?

Homework

- o If you are a member of small Christian community, give thanks to the Lord and renew your commitment.

- o If you are not part of a small Christian community, during your prayer time, ask the Lord to show you how He wants you to find community.

EVANGELIZATION

We must organize for justice. We must labor for peace. We must lobby for life. We must reach out and serve all those in need – the hungry, the lonely, the alienated, the sick, the imprisoned, the abandoned, the despairing, the addicted. The list is long. But, while all these are imperative to our mission from the Lord, one ministry stands first, head and shoulders above the rest: evangelization.

– Fr. Bob Bedard, CC

Personal Testimony

"Modern man listens more willingly to witnesses than to teachers, and if he does listen to teachers, it is because they are witnesses."
— *Pope Paul VI, On Evangelization in the Modern World*

Scriptures

1 Peter 3:15-16 Always be ready to give an explanation to anyone who asks you for a reason for your hope, but do it with gentleness and reverence...

Acts 1:8 You will receive power when the Holy Spirit comes to you, and you will be my witnesses...

Revelation 12:11 They conquered him (the accuser) by the blood of the Lamb and by the word of their testimony.

Acts 22:1 My brothers and fathers, listen to what I (Paul) am about to say to you in my defense.

John 20:18 Mary of Magdala went and announced to the disciples, "I have seen the Lord."

Isaiah 55:10-11 Yet just as from the heavens the rain and snow come down and do not return there till they have watered the earth, making it fertile and fruitful... so shall my word be that goes forth from my mouth; it shall not return to me empty...

Key Points

1. Your testimony is the most important tool in your evangelization tool box (Patti Mansfield).

2. Testimony: An explanation of how God has worked in your life.

3. Various types: personal conversion, baptism in the Holy Spirit, vocation, healing, growth in prayer.

4. Personal testimony is non-threatening, speaks for itself, and is hard to argue with.

5. Your encounter with the Lord might be exactly what someone needs to hear. It does not need to be spectacular.

6. Spend your whole life sharing your testimony!

Practical Application

1. Something supernatural happens when we share our testimony.

2. Taking time to write your testimony is one of the best investments you'll ever make.

3. Your testimony should be like a favorite poem or your best-hit song.

Discussion Questions

1. What is your testimony? (You can use the testimony worksheet on the next page.)

2. Do you sometimes share your testimony?

3. Do you have a conversion Scripture?

Homework

o Write a testimony that you can give in 3 minutes.

o Share your testimony with someone.

o Pray and journal about one key Scripture that relates to your testimony.

Testimony Worksheet

Life Before

Point of Conversion / Decision / God's Intervention

Life After

Basic Gospel Message

"There is no true evangelization if the name, the teaching, the life, the promises, the Kingdom and the mystery of Jesus of Nazareth, the Son of God are not proclaimed."
— *Pope Paul VI, On Evangelization in the Modern World*

Scriptures

John 3:16 For God so loved the world that He gave His only Son, so that everyone who believes in Him might not perish but might have eternal life.

Matthew 11:28 Come to Me, all you who labor and are burdened, and I will give you rest.

John 14:6 I am the way and the truth and the life. No one comes to the Father except through me.

John 6:37 I will not reject anyone who comes to me.

John 1:12 But to those who did accept him, he gave power to become children of God, to those who believe in his name.

Acts 4:12 There is no salvation through anyone else, nor is there any other name under heaven given to the human race by which we are to be saved.

Key Points

1. "Gospel" means "Good News"

2. The Gospel is not simply a call to live a religious and moral life; it's a call to encounter the Risen Savior.

3. Every Christian should be able to share the "Good News."

A way of summarizing the Good News

I.   God made you and loves you unconditionally.

II.   We are wounded and in need of a Savior.

III. God so loved the world that He gave His Son.

IV.   Jesus died so that we could have eternal life.

V.   Jesus is knocking at the door of our hearts.

VI.   We need to believe, repent, love and surrender.

VII. God will give us the power of the Holy Spirit.

VIII. We are called to be part of a family: the Church.

Another simpler summary: "Come to Me!"

And one more: "Jesus is alive!"

Practical Application

1. Christianity is all about relationship.

2. When we share our faith with others, it is important to get to the heart of the matter.

Discussion Questions

1. Could you summarize the Good News in your own words?

2. Have you ever shared the Good News with someone?

3. What part of the Good News might be hardest for someone to accept?

Homework

o Ponder the 8-point Good News summary (above) during one of your prayer times this week.

o Memorize one Scripture relating to the Good News.

Evangelization

"Though it is true that this mission demands great generosity on our part, it would be wrong to see it as a heroic individual undertaking, for it is first and foremost the Lord's work, surpassing anything which we can see and understand. Jesus is "the first and greatest evangelizer".
— *Pope Francis in "The Joy of the Gospel"*

Scriptures

Mark 16:15-16 Go into the whole world and proclaim the gospel to every creature. Whoever believes and is baptized will be saved; whoever does not believe will be condemned.

1 Corinthians 9:6 If I preach the gospel, this is no reason for me to boast, for an obligation has been imposed on me, and woe to me if I do not preach it!

Luke 4:18 The Spirit of the Lord is upon me, because he has anointed me to bring glad tidings to the poor.

2 Timothy 4:2 Proclaim the word; be persistent whether it is convenient or inconvenient; convince, reprimand, encourage through all patience and teaching.

Luke 9:26 Whoever is ashamed of me and my words, the Son of Man will be ashamed of when he comes in his glory and in the glory of the Father and of the holy angels.

Leviticus 19:16 You shall not stand by idly when your neighbor's life is at stake.

2 Corinthians 5:14 For the love of Christ impels us.

Key Points

1. We are all called to the Great Commission.

2. Evangelization is like one poor beggar telling another poor beggar that he found bread!

3. Every ministry we do should be evangelistic.

4. Evangelization should always lead to "letting the Lion out of the cage." It is important to actually pray with the person to encounter Jesus.

5. The Holy Spirit is essential for true evangelization.

6. When we evangelize, we proclaim to others: "Something happened to me. I'm not saying I'm better than you, but I know I am now a different and better person."

Practical Application

1. The work of evangelization is like building a cathedral; there are many different tasks and each must make a contribution.

2. Consider your own evangelistic tract.

Discussion Questions

1. Have you felt the call to the Great Commission?

2. What kind of evangelization work inspires you / intimidates you?

3. Do you have a favorite evangelization approach and Scripture?

Homework

- o Journal about how the Lord is calling you to evangelize.

- o Pray about your own evangelization Scripture.

- o Share your evangelization Scripture with at least one person.

Apologetics

"An argument in apologetics, when actually used in dialogue, is an extension of the arguer. The arguer's tone, sincerity, care, concern, listening, and respect matter as much as his or her logic – probably more. The world was won for Christ not by arguments but by sanctity: 'What you are speaks so loud, I can hardly hear what you say.'"

— *Peter Kreeft, Pocket Handbook of Christian Apologetics*

Scriptures

John 14:6 I am the way and the truth and the life. No one comes to the Father except through me.

John 8:12 I am the light of the world. Whoever follows me will not walk in darkness, but will have the light of life.

1 Peter 3:15-16 Always be ready to give an explanation to anyone who asks you for a reason for your hope, but do it with gentleness and reverence.

Galatians 2:2 I went up in accord with a revelation, and I presented to them the gospel that I preached to the Gentiles – but privately to those of repute – so that I might not be running, or have run, in vain.

Acts 15:1-2 Some who had come down from Judea were instructing the brothers, "Unless you are circumcised according to the Mosaic practice, you cannot be saved." Because there was no little dissension and debate by Paul and Barnabas with them, it was decided that Paul, Barnabas, and some of the others should go up to Jerusalem to the apostles and presbyters about this question.

Luke 20:27, 37 Some Sadducees, those who deny that there is a resurrection, came forward and put this question to Him... (Jesus:)That the dead will rise even Moses made know...

Ephesians 4:15 (RSV) Rather, speaking the truth in love...

Key Points

1. Apologetics is not apologizing for your faith but rather giving a reasonable explanation for your faith.

2. Jesus had to do apologetics. So do we. (What are questions we get asked?)

3. The world of apologetics is vast. Most of us wish we didn't have to do apologetics.

4. We need to learn our faith.

5. The truth will set people free but they need to be open-minded and open hearted.

6. Catholics do not believe in relativism. The Church has settled some questions so that we can get on with our lives.

7. What unites us is greater than what separates us.

8. It's okay to say: "I don't know, but I can find out for you."

9. Knowing our history is important. Pope Leo wrote: "The first law of history is not to dare to tell a lie; and the second, not to fear to tell the truth."

Practical Application

1. As Christians we need to be on going learners, not just for ourselves but also for others.

2. Learning our faith helps make it stronger.

Discussion Questions

1. Is there a teaching of the Church that you have studied and can explain to others?

2. What is a Church teaching that you would like to come to understand more deeply?

3. Have you ever helped someone to understand an element of the Catholic faith?

Homework

- o Read through the apologetics cheat sheet.
- o Choose one area of Catholic apologetics to study more deeply.

Mission

Quo Vadis?
— Where are you going?

Scriptures

Jeremiah 29:11 For I know well the plans I have in mind for you – oracle of the Lord – plans for your welfare and not for woe, so as to give you a future of hope.

Psalms 37:4 Find your delight in the Lord, who will give you your heart's desire.

Ezekiel 3:17 Son of man, I have appointed you a sentinel for the house of Israel.

John 21:17 Do you love me?... Feed my sheep!

1 Corinthians 9:16 If I preach the gospel, this is no reason for me to boast, for an obligation has been imposed on me, and woe to me if I do not preach it!

Philippians 3:13-14 ...forgetting what lies behind but straining forward to what lies ahead, I continue my pursuit toward the goal, the prize of God's upward calling, in Christ Jesus.

2 Timothy 4:7 I have competed well; I have finished the race, I have kept the faith.

Key Points

1. People who set goals and accomplish them are happy.

2. God made us for a purpose.

3. To discover your mission is to discover a treasure.

4. We are called to make the most of the gifts we have been given.

5. Our mission is unique, unrepeatable, and desperately needed in this world.

6. Who we become is far more important than what we do.

7. Having a personal mission statement is part of the Church's tradition. Example: priests, bishops, and communities.

Practical Application

1. Ask God to reveal to you your life's mission.

2. Write it down so that it is clear.

3. Learn to break big goals down into a series of small easy to achieve goals.

Discussion Questions

1. Are you a goal-oriented person?

2. Do you have a personal mission statement?

3. Is there a saint who inspires you in a special way?

Homework

- o Journal about goals: life, decade, year, quarter, month, etc.

- o Start a dream list in your journal.

- o Pray and journal about a life Scripture.

Seven Prayers Every Catholic Should Pray Every Day

Daily Offering

O my Jesus, through the Immaculate Heart of Mary, I offer You all my prayers, works, joys, and sufferings of this day, in union with the Holy Sacrifice of the Mass throughout the world, in thanksgiving for Your goodness to me, in reparation for my sins, for the intentions of my family and friends, and those who have asked me to pray for them, and for our Holy Father, the Pope. Amen.

Act of Contrition

O my God, I am heartily sorry for having offended You, and I detest all my sins, because I dread the loss of heaven, and the pains of hell; but most of all because they offend You, my God, Who are all good and deserving of all my love. I firmly resolve, with the help of Your grace, to confess my sins, to do penance, and to amend my life. Amen.

Our Father

Our Father, Who art in heaven, hallowed be Thy Name. Thy Kingdom come. Thy Will be done, on earth as it is in Heaven.

Give us this day our daily bread. And forgive us our trespasses, as we forgive those who trespass against us. And lead us not into temptation, but deliver us from evil. Amen.

Hail Mary

Holy Mary, Full of Grace, the Lord is with thee. Blessed art thou among women, and blessed is the fruit of thy womb, Jesus.

Holy Mary, Mother of God, pray for us our sinners, now and at the hour of our death. Amen.

Glory Be

Glory be to the Father, and to the Son, and to the Holy Spirit. As it was in the beginning, is now, and ever shall be, world without end. Amen.

Guardian Angel

Angel of God, my guardian dear, to whom God's love, commits me here. Ever this day, be at my side, to light and guard, to rule and guide. Amen.

Saint Michael the Archangel Prayer

Saint Michael the Archangel, defend us in battle. Be our defense against the wickedness and snares of the devil. May God rebuke him, we humbly pray, and do thou, O Prince of the heavenly hosts, by the power of God, thrust into hell Satan, and all the evil spirits, who prowl about the world seeking the ruin of souls. Amen.

Dates for Entrustment to St. Joseph

Feast	Start Day	Feast Day (Entrustment Day)
Saint Joseph, Husband of the Blessed Virgin Mary	Mar 10	March 19, 2019*
St. Joseph the Worker	Apr 22	May 01, 2019 *+
Holy Family	Dec 20	December 29, 2019*

* *Special Entrustment Ceremony at Catholic Charismatic Center (CCC), Houston, TX*

+ *On April 30th, 2019 (Vigil of St. Joseph the Worker), CCC will have a special celebration with entrustment to St. Joseph.*

Dates for Taking Mary Into Your Home

Choose one Feast Day and start preparing yourself for entrustment to Our Blessed Virgin Mary on its 'Start Day':

Feast	Start Day	Feast Day (Entrustment Day)
Mary, Mother of God	Dec 23	Jan 01
Presentation of the Lord	Jan 24	Feb 02
Our Lady of Lourdes	Feb 02	Feb 11
Annunciation of the Lord	Mar 16	March 25
Our Lady of Fatima	May 4	May 13
Visitation of the Blessed Virgin Mary	May 22	May 31
Mary, Mother of the Church	Jun 01	June 10th, 2019
Our Lady of Perpetual Help	Jun 18	June 27*
Our Lady of Mount Carmel	Jul 07	July 16*
Assumption of the Blessed Virgin Mary	Aug 06	August 15*
Our Lady of Sorrows	Sept 06	September 15*

Our Lady of the Miraculous Medal	*Nov 18*	*November 27*
Our Lady of Kibeho	*Nov 19*	*November 28*
Immaculate Conception of the Blessed Virgin Mary	*Nov 29*	*December 8**
Our Lady of Guadalupe	*Dec 03*	*December 12**

* Special ceremony at Catholic Charismatic Center, Houston, TX

CALENDAR

January 2019

S	M	T	W	Th	F	S
		1	2	3	4	5
6	7	8	9	10	11	12
13	14	15	16	17	18	19
20	21	22	23	24	25	26
27	28	29	30	31		

February 2019

S	M	T	W	Th	F	S
					1	2
3	4	5	6	7	8	9
10	11	12	13	14	15	16
17	18	19	20	21	22	23
24	25	26	27	28		

March 2019

S	M	T	W	Th	F	S
					1	2
3	4	5	6	7	8	9
10	11	12	13	14	15	16
17	18	19	20	21	22	23
24	25	26	27	28	29	30
31						

April 2019

S	M	T	W	Th	F	S
	1	2	3	4	5	6
7	8	9	10	11	12	13
14	15	16	17	18	19	20
21	22	23	24	25	26	27
28	29	30				

May 2019

S	M	T	W	Th	F	S
			1	2	3	4
5	6	7	8	9	10	11
12	13	14	15	16	17	18
19	20	21	22	23	24	25
26	27	28	29	30	31	

June 2019

S	M	T	W	Th	F	S
						1
2	3	4	5	6	7	8
9	10	11	12	13	14	15
16	17	18	19	20	21	22
23	24	25	26	27	28	29
30						

July 2019

S	M	T	W	Th	F	S
	1	2	3	4	5	6
7	8	9	10	11	12	13
14	15	16	17	18	19	20
21	22	23	24	25	26	27
28	29	30	31			

August 2019

S	M	T	W	Th	F	S
				1	2	3
4	5	6	7	8	9	10
11	12	13	14	15	16	17
18	19	20	21	22	23	24
25	26	27	28	29	30	31

September 2019

S	M	T	W	Th	F	S
1	2	3	4	5	6	7
8	9	10	11	12	13	14
15	16	17	18	19	20	21
22	23	24	25	26	27	28
29	30					

October 2019

S	M	T	W	Th	F	S
		1	2	3	4	5
6	7	8	9	10	11	12
13	14	15	16	17	18	19
20	21	22	23	24	25	26
27	28	29	30	31		

November 2019

S	M	T	W	Th	F	S
					1	2
3	4	5	6	7	8	9
10	11	12	13	14	15	16
17	18	19	20	21	22	23
24	25	26	27	28	29	30

December 2019

S	M	T	W	Th	F	S
1	2	3	4	5	6	7
8	9	10	11	12	13	14
15	16	17	18	19	20	21
22	23	24	25	26	27	28
29	30	31				

CERTIFICATE CHECKLIST

Daily Prayer

(Signature)

New Testament

- Matthew
- Mark
- Luke
- John
- Acts of the Apostles
- Romans
- 1 Corinthians
- 2 Corinthians
- Galatians

- Ephesians
- Philippians
- Colossians
- 1 Thessalonians
- 2 Thessalonians
- 1 Timothy
- 2 Timothy
- Titus
- Philemon

- Hebrews
- James
- 1 Peter
- 2 Peter
- 1 John
- 2 John
- 3 John
- Jude
- Revelation

(Signature)

Living Sacramental Life of the Church

(Signature)

"Mary in Your Home" novena

(Signature)

"Saint Joseph the Protector" novena

(Signature)

Foundations Series
Leader's Initials ＿＿＿

Living in the Spirit Series
Leader's Initials ＿＿＿

Evangelization Series
Leader's Initials ＿＿＿

Faith into Fire
Completion Date ＿＿＿＿＿＿＿
Leader's Initials ＿＿＿

Retreat
Completion Date ＿＿＿＿＿＿＿
Leader's Initials ＿＿＿

Conference
Completion Date ＿＿＿＿＿＿＿
Leader's Initials ＿＿＿

Christian Community
Name/Type _____

Leader's Initials _____

Charisms Workshop
Completion Date _____

Leader's Initials _____

YEAR OF THE LORD
Certificate in Christian Discipleship

DISCIPLE FORMATION SERIES SCHEDULE

FOUNDATIONS series
1.
2.
3.
4.
5.

LIVING IN THE SPIRIT series
1.
2.
3.
4.
5.

EVANGELIZATION series
1.
2.
3.
4.
5.

OTHER IMPORTANT DATES

Date of Assemblies:
1.
2.
3.

Graduation Ceremony:

Faith in the Fire retreat:

Charisms Workshop:

Entrustment to St. Joseph
Beginning date:
Consecration date:

Taking Mary into Your Home
Beginning date:
Consecration date:

Final Exam When We Die

The teaching ministry of Jesus ends and is perhaps summarized with *"The Judgment of the Nations"* (Matthew 25:31-46). This narrative closes with the verse: "And these will go off to eternal punishment, but the righteous to eternal life" (verse 46). It seems as though Jesus is revealing to us the questions we will be asked when we come before the judgment seat of God. Try to do each one of the things in the list below at least once this year:

- ❏ *I was hungry and did you give Me food?*
- ❏ *I was thirsty and did you give Me drink?*
- ❏ *A stranger and did you welcome Me?*
- ❏ *Naked and did you clothe Me?*
- ❏ *Ill and did you care for Me?*
- ❏ *In prison and did you visit Me?*

Vocabulary of Praise

I love You	I bless You	I worship You
I praise You	I adore You	I magnify You
I thank You	I desire You	I trust in You
I seek You	I hope in You	I long for You
I bow before You	I glory in You	I thirst for You
I exalt You	Alleluia	Holy is the Lord
Praise the Lord	Glory to God in the Highest	

Titles of Jesus: "You are (my)…" "I love You (my)…"

Redeemer	Savior
Deliverer	Healer
Son of God	Prince of Peace
Bread of Life	King of kings
Name above all names	Light of the World
Word made Flesh	Lord of lords
Good Shepherd	Messiah
My Life and my Love	Alpha and Omega

Attributes of God: "You are…"

Holy	Awesome	True
Steadfast	Loving	Merciful
Glorious	Mighty	A Just Judge
Beautiful	Good	Tender-Hearted
Faithful and Just	Forgiving	True to Your word

Attributes of God in relation to us: "You are…"

My Rock	My Refuge	My Strength
My Glory	My Portion and Cup	My Joy
My Healer	My God and My All	My Hiding Place
My Defense	My Treasure	My Father
My Provider	My Salvation	My Sanctification

Worship Songs

Alpha and Omega

You are Alpha and Omega!
We worship You, our Lord.
You are worthy to be praised.
>We give You all the glory!
>We worship you, our Lord,
>You are worthy to be praised.

"Alpha and Omega" By Erasmus Mutanbira / © 2005 Integrity's Praise! Music (Admin. by Capitol CMG Publishing (Integrity Music [DC Cook])) / Sound Of The New Breed (Admin. by Capitol CMG Publishing (Integrity Music [DC Cook])) / CCL # 1518894

Bless The Lord

Bless the Lord O my soul!
O my soul! Worship His holy name.
Sing like never before, O my soul!
I'll worship Your holy name.

"10,000 Reasons (Bless The Lord)" By Jonas Myrin and Matt Redman / © 2011 Atlas Mountain Songs (Admin. by Capitol CMG Publishing) / sixsteps Music (Admin. by Capitol CMG Publishing) / Thankyou Music (Admin. by Capitol CMG Publishing) / worshiptogether.com songs (Admin. by Capitol CMG Publishing) / CCL # 1518894

I Give You My Heart

Lord, I give You my heart. I give You my soul.
I live for You alone. Every breath that I take,
every moment I'm awake, Lord have Your way in me.

"I Give You My Heart" By Reuben Morgan / © 1995 Hillsong Music Publishing (Admin. by Capitol CMG Publishing) / CCL # 1518894

Sanctuary

Lord prepare me to be a sanctuary,
pure and holy tried and true.
With thanksgiving, I'll be a living sanctuary for You.

Send Down Fire!

Send down fire! The Holy Ghost Fire!
Send down fire again! The Holy Ghost fire!

The Lord Has Made This Day

The Lord has made this day let us rejoice
The Lord has made this day Amen. Amen.

They Prayed, They Sang

They prayed, they sang
The Holy Ghost came down! (repeat)

The Wall of Jericho

The wall of Jericho fell down flat!
The wall of Jericho fell down flat!
When the children of God were praising the Lord,
The wall of Jericho fell down flat!

"Send Down Fire!", "The Lord Has Made This Day", "They Prayed, They Sang", and "The Wall of
Jericho" are Nigerian songs and melody.

As I Kneel Before You

Maria Parkinson

As I kneel before you,
As I bow my head in prayer,
Take this day, make it yours
And fill me with your love.

Refrain:
Ave Maria, gratia plena
Dominus tecum, benedicta tu.

All I have I give you,
Every dream and wish are yours.
Mother of Christ, Mother of mine,
Present them to my Lord.

As I kneel before you
And I see your smiling face,
Every thought, every word
Is lost in your embrace.

As I walk beside you
And I hold your hand in mine,
Mother of God, show me the way
And lead me to your Son.

Made in the USA
Middletown, DE
27 December 2020